Asking God

Also in this same series

Each Day, Each Night   Paul Sheppey

Rhythms of Prayer   Raymond Chapman

Asking God

a pocket book of intercessions

Oliver S. Tomkins

CANTERBURY
PRESS
Norwich

First published in 1998 by The Canterbury Press Norwich
(a publishing imprint of Hymns Ancient & Modern Limited,
a registered charity)
St Mary's Works, St Mary's Plain
Norwich, Norfolk, NR3 3BH

© Deborah Page 1998

British Library Cataloguing in Publication Data

A catalogue record for this book is available
from the British Library

ISBN 1-85311-200-3

*Typeset by David Gregson Associates, Beccles, Suffolk
Printed and bound in Great Britain by
Redwood Books, Trowbridge, Wiltshire*

Contents

Day	Morning	Evening	
I	Leaders	Fruits of the Spirit: Love	2
2	Government	Fruits of the Spirit: Joy	4
3	Work	Fruits of the Spirit: Peace	6
4	Administration	Fruits of the Spirit: Patience	8
5	Families in Need	Fruits of the Spirit: Kindness	10
6	The Arts	Fruits of the Spirit: Goodness	12
7	The Sciences	Fruits of the Spirit: Faithfulness	14

About the Author

Oliver Tomkins (1908–1992)

Oliver Tomkins was, he often liked to remark, a 'both–and' person, not an 'either–or' one. He felt at home with many traditions and experiences; he was both by temperament and by conviction inclusive, not exclusive. Clinging to 'both–and' is not always the best way of coping intellectually or practically with the sort of challenge that requires a choice (and Oliver did, of course, recognize that choices do have to be made) but it may provide the best grounding for prayer, which needs to be large in its sympathies, all embracing in its objects, and open to the incomprehensible vastness of the love of God. Oliver was a good pray-er. Man of action as he was, prayer always came first, and his regular prayer-time at the beginning of the day was enormously important. Born in China, the child of Congregationalist missionaries, Oliver became an Anglican priest, a leading activist in the ecumenical movement, a parish priest in Sheffield, principal of a theological college in Lincoln and Bishop of Bristol. He was a man for many seasons but perhaps at his very best in the long maturity of his retirement at Worcester.

There is a lovely picture of his grandfather, Daniel Tomkins, a Gladstonian Free Churchman, full of kindness and good works, sitting contentedly in his garden in old age with his dog beside him. It was painted by no one less than Alfred Munnings, when still young and almost unknown. Oliver loved that picture. It expressed a mature harmony of nature and grace. Even more did he love Andrei Rublev's wonderful icon of the Holy Trinity with the three angelic figures, expressive of an extraordinarily powerful sense of supernatural serenity, surrounding the cup and bread of life. A copy of this icon was always with him: in his chapel as bishop, in his study in retirement, and finally at his memorial service. Such were some of the images which moved his heart.

Oliver was very tall but his towering above others never seemed competitive. He was indeed the least competitive of people, always more a listener than a speaker. An Anglican through and through, he never lost the Congregationalist affections of his family tradition, but he loved no less the wealth of spiritual things to be found in the Roman Catholic Church. A good friend of that pioneer of spiritual ecumenism, the Abbé Paul Couturier, who began the January Octave of Prayer for Christian Unity, Oliver loved to wear the beret, characteristic of every French Catholic priest, which Couturier had given him.

Oliver was Assistant General Secretary of the World Council of Churches during its crucial formative years, just after the Second World War. He had responsibility for its 'Faith and Order' side and, in 1964, presided over the British 'Faith and Order' conference at Nottingham, the only really major ecumenical conference that the churches in Britain have ever held. The early 1960s were a heady time and the Nottingham commitment to achieving full visible unity by 1980 was not destined to be achieved, any more than was Anglican–Methodist unity, another cause Oliver had striven hard to bring about. Nor, by only a matter of days, did he live to see his own church's acceptance of the ordination of women, something particularly close to his heart.

All of this and much else fed into Oliver's prayer life and into the innumerable prayers, personal and public, he addressed to God. Many of them are very shareable and just because he himself was so open to the worries and, needs of others, it seems absolutely right that a selection of them should now be printed for use by the wider congregation of men and women, in all churches and none, that he served so generously.

Adrian Hastings
November 1997

Adrian Hastings, former Professor of Theology at the University of Leeds, is the author of a forthcoming biography of Oliver Tomkins.

Introduction

Oliver Tomkins wrote this collection of prayers over decades; they are the fruit of a lifetime and can be read and re-read, prayed again and again. He kept them in a loose-leaf pocket book and the monthly cycle followed here is his own. He used these prayers of intercession and petition, together with systematic lists of people and situations, in the context of the daily office of Morning and Evening Prayer.

Intercession is prayer for, with and on behalf of others; it is when we place ourselves between God and the world. Oliver's prayers remind us that intercession should not be partisan, but rather demands a solidarity with the world. He prays for the whole: the whole community, the whole nation, the whole world. Petition concerns our straight course to God, and recognizes our dependence on him. In these prayers Oliver dwells on aspects of the nature of God, acknowledges by contrast the degree to which we fall short of these, and then confidently asks God to conform us to his image. Thus we are led from self-obsession to transfiguration.

These prayers can be used either privately or in public worship. They are not offered as a complete diet, but for use alongside other forms of prayer. Not all of the prayers set for any one day are intended for use at once. Rather, you may like to relish and take time to focus on one or two; otherwise spiritual indigestion may ensue! Following themes through consecutive days, be they the Beatitudes, Gifts of the Spirit or whatever, allows something quite familiar to address us afresh, just as we are led beyond and behind the familiar in Oliver's meditations on the Lord's Prayer.

Prayer in the Bible is characterized by the memory of God's saving acts in the past, by a trust that he is present in the difficulties and joys of life, and by a hopeful expectation that the broken distortions of life will not have the final word. Much of *our* prayer backs away from that sort of clarity and honesty; we feel that we should be more sophisticated in our prayers. Simple asking can often feel unworthy. This collection restores our confidence in prayer as asking. It shows us how, by regular prayer, our way of looking at the world changes and grows. The rhythm of faithful prayer itself moves us to recognize what questions we should ask.

For Oliver, daily prayer was an essential. It was a heartfelt and thoughtful business that restored the imbalances of life, because it caught a glimpse of the proper relationship of creature to Creator. These prayers can heal us, by simply leading us to a sense of thankfulness and trust. They are the prayers of a thankful soul; thankful for God being God; thankful for the spectrum of people and activities in creation; thankful for a Church he longed to see united yet which, even in its brokenness, refracted Christ's beauty. He constantly updated and added to his prayers. They inevitably reflect his own concerns and are signposts to his life, but also to a way of praying which we can share. He is a compassionate, experienced guide, and we are privileged to benefit from his journey, wisdom, victories and defeats. His openness gives us the courage to voice for ourselves what we must say: to pray as we can. We can pray these prayers as they stand, but also alter and add to them until they become truly our own, perhaps even taking them into a prayer cycle of our own making. Above all, Oliver wanted people to have the confidence to pray authentically for themselves. May these prayers help others to pray.

Deborah Page (née Tomkins) and Andrew Teal.
November 1997

Deborah Page is Oliver Tomkins' youngest daughter.

Andrew Teal is Vicar of St Mary, Tickhill with Stainton in the Diocese of Sheffield.

Preface

Prayer includes asking, although it includes much more.

These little prayers have grown, over the years, from seeking to put into words, after other facets of prayer have had their place, some *asking* which this child of God, at any rate, wanted to bring to the Father.

They seek, by intercession and petition, to help stretch my narrow prayers towards the width of God's concerns; to intercede, as the days of the month come round, for a wide range of God's children as I know them; to ask, for myself and for others, those gifts and graces through which God draws us to himself, and, by his Spirit, forms Christ in us, the hope of glory.

I have found that it helps me to pray to write down some of my prayers. The only point in sharing these is the hope that it may encourage you to try the same.

Oliver Tomkins

Day One ✳ Morning

Leaders

Heads of state

O God, we thank you that our experience of sovereignty suggests words and feelings with which to approach you, and that our awe before your majesty illuminates the mystery of human power.

We pray for all those in whom is focused the rule of their peoples and who know the loneliness of that calling.

We pray especially for Elizabeth our Queen, that she may keep alive in our hearts the sense of awe in the face of greatness, and that she herself may be sustained under the heavy weight of duty by communion with an almighty power which is also a father's love, made clear in Jesus Christ our Lord.

The Prime Minister

O God, whom to serve is to reign, we pray for *Name* our Prime Minister in the loneliness of being chief servant of our nation, that he/she may be strengthened by trust in you and by our trust in him/her, for Christ's sake.

Day One ☽ *Evening*

Fruits of the Spirit – Love

Love

God, grant me love, and then love, and then love, and then love … until I no longer know that I lack it.

Agape

O God, you gave your Church a new experience for which they had to mint a new word. Help us in our generation to see vividly the daily newness of your love and to greet you, and each other, in joyful surprise.

The cost of love

Father of Christ crucified, to love is to be vulnerable;
Father of Christ risen, to love is to be victorious.
Give us grace not to expect the victory without the wounds, for his sake by whose wounds we are healed.

Focusing on God

Father, grant me that focusing of all desire which is the mark of being in love, undistracted by all lesser impulses, so that my longing is pure, for you alone. Then, may I see you as you are.

Day Two ✳ Morning

Government

Politicians

O God, in whom alone truth and power are perfectly united, we pray for your blessing upon those who must please many if they are to succeed, yet must love truth if they are to deserve our trust. Shield them from corruption by power and shield us from fear of truth, that we may wish our rulers to be that which you also desire, for Christ's sake.

Christian politicians

Heavenly Father, we pray especially for those politicians who consciously submit their decisions to your will made known in Christ, for we guess that in doing so they share a little in his crucifixion. He, too, got caught between those who were zealous for the causes they believed in and those who would always play for safety. So grant them the comfort of forgiveness when they are mistaken, of a quiet spirit when they follow conscience and of the knowledge of our prayers at all times, for Christ's sake.

One-party States

Lord have mercy on those who rule whilst unable to trust in the consent of their people. Grant them so to rule that they may come to be trusted, for everyone's sake.

Day Two ● Evening

Fruits of the Spirit – Joy

Joy

Father of light and life, I give you thanks for the surprise of joy; keep me always open to spontaneity, ready to be captured by rapture, and in it to recognize the spark that leaps from Creator to creature.

The thing in itself

God the Creator, give me grace to enjoy things for their own sake, to contemplate simply the thing in itself. Nothing I can touch or see is unworthy of wonder: the infinite varieties of texture, the mystery of colour and light, the receding of worlds of microscopic being, the subtle relations between parts and whole.

Lead me, Lord, down all these paths of joy, my hand in yours, so that I do not forget whose work they are.

Going to church

Father of all Christian worshippers, forgive us that few would guess from our behaviour in church that love and joy are chief among the fruits of the Spirit. Grant that when we worship, our hearts if not our bodies may dance and our spirits jump for joy. 'Endue thy ministers with righteousness: and make thy chosen people joyful!'

Day Three ✳ *Morning*

Work

Employers and employed

God of justice, we pray for those who have long fought for their rights, that they and their families may be gladly given the rewards which they deserve. Help employers and employed to see the whole picture, with themselves as part of it; for the sake of him who taught us to go beyond justice into generosity, your Son Jesus, our Lord.

The unemployed

Father forgive us that we condemn some of our fellows to an enforced leisure which marks them as unwanted. Give them inner resources of self-respect and hope, and grant to us corporately some solution which leaves no one feeling 'redundant'. For pity's sake, whose name is Jesus.

Difficult jobs

God, we pray for those who do the dirty or dangerous jobs which we are glad to avoid. As we stay warm and clean, let us remember gratefully those who dig coal, empty dustbins, clean our streets and buildings, and the like; and let me get *my* hands dirty often enough not to feel that I live in a completely different world. For Jesus' sake, whose incarnation made him the servant of all.

Fruits of the Spirit – Peace

Peace

God, give me your peace so that I may radiate it, for the sake of Jesus, who offers his peace as he receives it from you, and for the sake of all people, who need the peace which only you can give.

Armaments and peace

O God, we know there are wicked people in the world, since we are among them. You know there are wicked people in the world, since the one time you really showed your face we killed you.

Forgive us that we need to retain weapons because we cannot trust each other.

Forgive us that we retain weapons which it would be blasphemy ever to use.

Grant us grace to trust each other enough to reduce our wicked stocks of death.

Grant us grace to trust you enough to risk crucifixion.

Because you accepted the risk and paid the full price, grant us repentance before we die and before we kill each other and all creation, and urgently, for dear Christ's sake.

Administration

Civil servants

Father, who alone can care for all while caring for each, grant your grace to those whose duty it is to deal impersonally with vast numbers of people, that they may always see the human being behind the number or inside the file, a person like themselves, for Christ's sake.

Strengthen with love those who deal daily with insoluble problems, who live continually before the bottomless pit of human need. Save them from cynicism or neurosis and grant them sufficient success to remain hopeful, O God of hope.

Monotonous work

God, you have set us to live in complex dependence on each other. Reward with the knowledge of our gratitude and your intimate care those who do what we are glad to avoid:

all who fill in forms and add up figures,
all who file and sort endless paper,
all who stay in back rooms that we may get out of doors.

Day Four ◐ *Evening*

Fruits of the Spirit – Patience

Patience

Father, keep me mindful of your readiness to be patient with me:

    your continued forgiveness for my monotonous sin,

    your standing back until I see something for myself,

    your tolerance of my limited gifts in the unlimited chances which you give me to use them,

and so much else which may remind me to be patient with others.

Long-suffering

Father, I often get impatient with those who are slower and more stupid than I am. I listen with difficulty to those who say only what I have heard a thousand times. Help me to remember always how you could be utterly bored by me, who am so slow to hear what you are saying and so quick to whine about the same old things: but, mercifully, you are not, because you are long-suffering. Teach me to be so, too.

Families in Need

One-parent families

God, you are Father and Mother to all your children, and from you all family life in heaven and earth is named. Be with those who are struggling to be both father and mother to their children and daily to make good the contribution of the missing partner. Grant them the extra insight, courage and love which they need, and draw them into such fellowship with you that they may find in you the full parental grace they need, O God our Father, Christ our Mother, and Spirit the bond of love, one God for ever.

Broken marriages

O God, they meant it when they said 'for better or for worse, until death us do part'. And now, is it a kind of spiritual death that has smitten them? Is there anything left alive which could rejoice again? If so, show it to them: guide them into peace and joy after such stress and pain. If not, let them bury their dead, in tears but not in bitterness.

Risen Lord, grant them somehow, somewhere, true experience of resurrection which, in you, is always a possibility.

Day Five ● Evening

Fruits of the Spirit – Kindness

Love is kind

O God, whose kindness to us is the measure of your love, grant us such love towards our neighbours that our sympathy stands us beside them to share their frailty, and that our kindness may be without condescension. For the sake of him who came to stand beside us, your incarnate Son, Jesus our Lord.

Cruel to be kind?

Kind Father, we thank you for every experience which only afterwards could be seen as a sign of your love. Give us grace to exercise that kindness which does not weaken those who receive it, and that humility which is not too quick to know what is good for others!

Kindness amidst conflict

God, we get caught in conflicts not of our making and in problems which others must solve; then we may do things out of group loyalty which we would not do as individuals. Bring shafts of light into this blackness by letting an individual here and there, act as if other individuals mattered most of all, for Christ's sake, who still gets hurt.

The Arts

God, creator of all loveliness and source of all being, give to the artists in every medium such skill in portraying reality that we may see that the artist's calling is to reflect yourself, in whom truth, beauty and goodness are fused.

Poets

God, open our ears to hear what the poets are saying. Since you have laid on them the burden of seeing deeper into truth than the rest of us, let us at least profit from their pain by listening to them.

Writers

'An author is a person who finds writing particularly difficult.' (Thomas Mann)
O God, strengthen those who struggle with words, that they may set free those which should live.

Frustrated artists

'When so many bad books get printed, why can't my bad book get printed?' (Thomas Merton)
God, you must know what it is like to fail to get a hearing, to create loveliness and to have it ignored. Stand beside those who feel frustrated that what cost so much to create cannot find an outlet – and teach them your endless patience.

Fruits of the Spirit – Goodness

Goodness

Father, make it my only ambition to be good: to be good with your goodness, which comes from you alone.

'Barnabas was a good man'
(Acts 11:24)

Father, you know there is no counterfeiting goodness, sheer goodness. We all recognize it and are glad. Thank you.

Thank goodness

Father, thank you for countless ways in which the goodness of others refreshes our lives:

    for the little acts of kindness,

    for the sympathetic smile,

    for the gestures of generosity,

    for every way in which your goodness is mediated,

for you, and you alone, are absolute goodness.

The saints

Father, I thank you for those I have known whom humility made so transparent that I saw you through them.

Day Seven ✳ Morning

The Sciences

Scientists

Your 'spacious firmament', O God, is more vast and complex than our forebears ever knew; our skills to measure and control it grow so fast that we think we are like gods. Bless those who concentrate upon 'how' and make them ask 'why' until they see 'who', through Jesus Christ our Lord.

The applied sciences

Grant, O Lord, to all who touch our daily lives with hard-won knowledge, that they may be as sensitive to beauty as they are to truth. Guide their consciences so that the release of power stored in nature may foster goodness in mankind.

Naturalists

Praise be to you, O God, for all who closely observe and accurately classify the infinite variety of nature. For it is part still of Adam's stewardship to name all creatures, so that, being better known, they may be better loved and more deeply revered, to the glory of their Maker.

Day Seven ☽ Evening

Fruits of the Spirit – Faithfulness

Faithfulness

Faithfulness means keeping promises: so when God seems not to keep his promises and our faith is stretched to breaking-point, we can only suppose that we misunderstood him.

O God, reassure those who feel they can no longer trust you. Take us by your Spirit into the secret counsels of the Father with the Son, where he who seemed so abandoned was able to accept his bitter cup and commend himself trustfully into your hands at the last.

Talents

'You have been faithful in small things …' (Matthew 25:14–30)
Almighty and generous Father, we thank you for the diversity of gifts with which you have entrusted us. Help us not to be envious that some have many and some have few, but grant to each of us so to use what we have that at last we may hear those longed-for words, 'Well done, good and faithful servant, enter into the joy of your Lord.'

Music and Drama

Musicians

Master of all music, help me to imagine a splendour of worship in which Mozart, Beethoven and Bach are but as the orchestra tuning up.

The gift of music

O God of infinite mystery, we marvel and rejoice that through the miracle of sound you reach those who do not know who is reaching them, but only that they have been outside themselves and have known ecstasy. Take away the veil, sometimes at least, that such as these may know whom to thank, for Christ's sake, your Son and your joy.

The drama of history

God, you are writing a play of which you let us catch glimpses.

In the beginning, God; creation is your unique handi-
work.

In the middle comes One who is the pivot, BC/AD;
that is the pattern of history.

In the end, God; however this story will end we
believe that it is in your hands, and that whatever
Jesus means is what the whole story means.

O God, it is a great drama in which you have called me to live my tiny part.

Fruits of the Spirit – Meekness

Sorry

Lord, grant me the spirit which, quite spontaneously, is ready to say 'sorry':

sorry – I was wrong,
sorry – I didn't mean that,
sorry – I simply forgot,
sorry – I ought to have thought of that,

instead of being instantly on the defensive.

Thoughtless words

'Set a watch, O Lord, before my mouth: and keep the door of my lips.' (Psalm 141:3)

O Lord, arrest before they get out the words

which will hurt the hearts or the names of others,
which are ugly, petty, dirty, shameful,
which I will long to recall, but will never be able,

and allow through only the ones which Jesus might have used, for his love's sake.

Day Nine ✷ Morning

The Media

The global village

O God, up until now only you have been able to bear knowing everything the moment it happens; have pity upon us who have now burdened ourselves with our instantaneous and universal awareness, beyond our capacity to feel or to understand. Lord have mercy – Christ have mercy – Lord have mercy; before the medium becomes the only message.

The effects of television

Heavenly Father, watch over the children who watch television. Let what should not stay wash over them; let images of beauty remain; save them from being trivialized by excess, from mistaking sensation for feeling and show them when to switch off.

Programme makers

Jesus, you know the cost of the Word becoming visible. Be present, as the Light which lightens everyone, with those who clothe ideas in speech and pictures. Make them sensitive to ways in which they will be understood; give them a care for truth above sensation, for beauty above horror and for goodness above 'news', so that neither their own souls nor ours may be damned by inadvertence, for your sake, who paid the price for our salvation.

Day Nine ☽ Evening

Cardinal Virtues – Temperance

Zealots

Lord Jesus, you called a zealot to be your disciple and then gave him a task which used all his heat to good effect. Bless all those who are red-hot in your service, that they may be consumed to your glory, and to the blessing and not the hurt of others. Grant more zeal to the temperate and more temperance to the zealous, that, between us, your kingdom may be widened on earth and our service accepted in heaven.

Brother Ass

(St Francis of Assisi's comic name for his body)

You must be treated kindly but firmly, I have no right to flog you and overdrive you, for God gave you to me to carry me to my journey's end on earth, whenever that may be. Nor must I indulge you, with too many carrots or too long in the straw, for then you and I will be delayed upon our master's business. I will try to keep you fit to carry me; you may not ask for more, but I owe you no less, until the time comes to enter Jerusalem.

Journalism

The Press

O God, deliver us from the abstract words that hide men and women behind a cloud; deliver us from the untrue words that value sensation more than the facts; deliver us from emotive words that rouse our feelings at the expense of our minds; and guard, through the Word himself, all those who follow the dangerous trade of dealing in words.

Unethical journalism

O God of truth and love, I find it hard to forgive those who smear the innocent with rumour, who invade the privacy of grief with prying, who exploit our worst passions for their own profit. Please grant us enough imagination to stop buying such stuff, and have mercy, for such nastiness lies within us all.

Foreign correspondents

O God, grant that nation may speak peace unto nation through the integrity of those who, from foreign soil, bear witness to their home country. We thank you for those who deepen our understanding of other nations and cultures so that sympathy may breed tolerance and tolerance breed peace. Arm them with truth, guard them from being misunderstood or misinterpreted, and protect them from the rancour of those whom they justly criticize.

Day Ten ◑ Evening

Cardinal Virtues – Prudence

Prudence is a virtue when it is the prelude to courage.

Prudence is the calculated choice between two risks.

Prudence is the bond of the other virtues: the insight to know the proportions in which they are to be practised.

Working out the cost

'What man, building a tower or going to war, does not sit down and work out the cost?' (Luke 14:28)
Lord, lead me into the adventures which prudence must estimate and grant me the prudence which embarking upon adventures demands. Save me from that parody of prudence which always hovers on the edge; save me from the lack of prudence which frustrates all completion by lack of resources.

Prudence

Lord, this is a more heroic virtue than at first appears! As I have seen it at work in others it was the hard-won fruit of a deep and patient discipline, getting the proportions right before embarking on decisive action. Thank you, Lord, for those who show it, and may there be many more.

The Vulnerable

Children and their carers

Lord Jesus, you had a special corner in your heart for children. You blessed them; you asked us all to learn from them; you burned with anger against those who caused them to stumble; you promised the care of guardian angels. All this you still do, for you are the same, yesterday, today and for ever.

Be close to those who now care for your little ones. Give to them your tenderness, and your sternness to those who threaten them, and watch over them with your protecting strength.

The elderly
(Luke 2:22–38)

O God, whose incarnate Son was greeted in babyhood by the insight of the aged, we praise you for Simeons and Annas everywhere, for their perception both of suffering and of joy, for their ripe fruit of holiness, for their patient waiting upon the Lord and for their readiness to depart in peace, having seen salvation in Christ, our Saviour.

Day Eleven ☽ *Evening*

Cardinal Virtues – Justice

Justice

Almighty God, Judge of all, have mercy upon us who have to make judgements upon our fellows. In the smallness of our hearts, love is too often a partial affection; in the smallness of our minds, knowledge is always imperfect, and yet we *must* decide. Forgive us when we are wrong, have mercy on us when we are right, lest we come to believe that it has been by our own wisdom; for Christ's sake.

The prayer of an administrator

God, you have given me a job in which I must take decisions which affect people's lives and happiness; the thought of them invades my mind incessantly. My prayers suddenly turn into committee meetings, as the pros and cons sway to and fro in argument. The most I can hope for is to be judged to have been just by those whose lives my decisions have touched. I can't ask their forgiveness, for the decisions had to be mine, but I can ask for yours. I do so now, in the prayer that when those in my charge cannot understand me, they may still trust me, because they believe that I trust in you.

Schools

Primary schools

God, help us to recognize the importance of early years,
  when emotions may be coloured for life,
  when trust or fear may become dominant,
  when the pattern of relationship with others is shaped,
and grant especial grace to those whom you have called to
teach children during such truly tender years.

Secondary schools

O God, grant us such concern for every child and such
insight as sees their gifts, that our schools may combine
equality with excellence in ways we have not yet
achieved, for Christ's sake.

The education system

O God of wisdom and power, be present by your Spirit
wherever decisions are taken about our children; keep the
politicians, the civil servants and the teachers' unions
sensitive to each other and, above all, mindful of the children they serve, lest they incur the judgement you
pronounced upon those who cause the little ones to
stumble, through Jesus Christ, who loves them all.

Day Twelve ◑ *Evening*

Cardinal Virtues – Fortitude

Fortitude

O God, give me guts. Only if I have the courage to go on, and then still go on when everything in me cries piteously to be allowed to stop, only *beyond* that point can I know the blessedness of being picked up, utterly exhausted, by the Good Shepherd.

The gift of tears

Lord, courage is good, but there comes a moment when it is better not to be brave. Grant, to those who need it, the gift of tears, when the price of being made whole is the admission of being broken.

Be of good courage ... fear not

O living, loving God, when my heart fails me
   for fear of loneliness, of dereliction by you and by my
      friends;
   for fear of your call to follow and the price for doing so;
   for fear of the weakness of my resources;
   for fear of death;
grant me to know by faith
   that you are there, I need only to wait;
   that my friends are there, ready to help;
   that you call me only to empower me for my calling
and that you have overcome death and wait for me.

Teachers

Teachers' ideals

Rabboni, teach us not to lose heart. You know how resistant we can all be; you know the heartbreak of seeing your teaching ignored. Grant to those who started teaching with high ideals that they may never cease to believe that it *can* work!

Teacher training

O God, teach the teachers your wisdom that they may be gentle with the backward, stimulating to the lively and loving to all, so that truth may be found to be exciting and goodness be found to be attractive, through him who was our teacher, Jesus Christ.

Understanding the whole

Heavenly Father, have mercy upon our shattered culture, our disintegration into specialisms which lack any overarching purpose, our feverish cleverness which does not recognize wisdom. Bring us through this dark age into your light, before we destroy ourselves, for the sake of Jesus, your uncompromising Truth.

Day Thirteen ☽ *Evening*

Theological Virtues – Faith

By faith

Father in heaven, give me the assurance of things hoped for, the conviction of things not seen, so that I may be among those who walk through this world in step with an unheard drum, who dance to an inaudible music – yet more real than the noises which constantly batter us.

Trust

Lord, does faith simply mean trust? Trusting you to be wholly loving, reliable, good? If so, then indeed I need to pray 'Lord, increase our faith'.

The 'proportions of the faith'
(Romans 12:6, Psalm 31:8)

Eternal God, 'thou has set our feet in a large room', help us to explore with expectant joy the wide spaces of faith:

go with us into the ages of history and the vistas of space – that we welcome what is, the facts outside us and the people who address us;

go with us on the adventures of the mind – for though we shall never know much, the quest for truth is what our minds are for;

be with us in the silence – when we withdraw into our innermost selves, when we search the furthest mystery, let us find you.

Higher Education

Students

God of all truth, give to those who seek, enough light to walk by; to those who believe, enough humility to know that there is more to be learned; and to all of us the faith that seeks understanding; through Jesus Christ who is himself the Way, the Truth, the Life.

Student chaplains

O God, who in Christ is both beside and beyond us, give to student chaplains the grace to be near enough those they serve to be trusted, and far enough ahead to be worth following, for the sake of that same Christ.

Researchers

God, the source and limit of all truth, go with all explorers into knowledge that they may travel towards you and be saved from falling into the abyss of untruth. Grant them the perseverance which waits for truth to show itself, the intuition which recognizes it before it vanishes, and reward them at the last with the knowledge of yourself, for Christ's sake.

Learning

'I believe that I may understand' – St Anselm.

O Lord, grant faith, that we may find meaning.

Day Fourteen ◐ Evening

Theological Virtues – Hope

Hope

Lord of all time and space, renew in a frightened and forgetful world the hope that springs from trusting your purpose in all things, that the kingdoms of this world shall become the kingdom of your Christ.

Hope for the world

O God, as we learn more about the infinite patience which has fashioned your creation, the microscopic detail, the countless millennia of evolution, open our eyes also to see the purpose to which all tends in Christ, Alpha and Omega, the beginning and the end. Thus may we live in a spirit of hope and transfigure the dangers and discouragements that come from taking a short term view. For Christ's sake, who is our hope.

The hope of glory

'We rejoice in our hope ... and hope does not disappoint us.'
(Romans 5:2–5)

Almighty God, by the resurrection of your Son, who was faithful to death, you brought into this world a new hope of life. Grant us to share his obedience that we may hope for his glory and not be disappointed.

Confirmation

Those to be confirmed

Defend, O Lord, these your children with your heavenly grace, that they may continue yours –

in the freshness of desire which moved them to be confirmed;

in the thirst for truth which preparation aroused;

in the sincerity with which they meant their promises;

– and in these gifts may they daily increase until they come to your everlasting kingdom.

After confirmation

'… continue thine forever'

Father, you see the sincerity which children bring to their confirmation; give to the local church which surrounds them the loving grace to sustain them in untarnished hope, for Christ's sake.

Adult confirmands

God, who gives by the Spirit the gifts

of wisdom and understanding,

of counsel and inward strength,

of knowledge and true godliness,

and of fear of the Lord;

grant that those who come to you in maturity may abide in you like children, and so enter your Kingdom.

Day Fifteen ◐ Evening

Theological Virtues – Charity

Charity

God, make me warm-hearted to my neighbours, and so influence me with your charity that I may love those whom I cannot like.

Fanatics

Lord, it is hard to pray for those who ruthlessly destroy others in the belief that their cause justifies it.

You manage to love the terrorists, the kidnappers of hostages, the suicide bombers, just as much as you love those whom they kill.

I can't manage it. All I feel able to do is to commend them into your keeping. You alone know what to do with them, for Christ's sake, who died for them too.

Openness
(Luke 9:49–50)

God of all goodness
      all truth
      all beauty
open our hearts to receive you and our eyes to see you when you arrive where we are not expecting you. Free us from the mean jealousy which tries to possess you and bring us face to face with Jesus, Lord of all.

Ministry

Training for the ordained ministry

Lord of the Church and Saviour of all, call to the Church's ministry those whom you want, and grant them the gifts which they need:

open their minds to truth and their hearts to love,

strengthen their wills to serve and their bodies to endure,

keep printed in their remembrance how great a treasure is committed to their charge,

through Jesus Christ our Lord.

Theologians

Father of light and truth, we praise you for those whose thinking brings light into obscure places and whose perception awakens response in our own minds. So guide and guard our theologians that they may not lead us astray nor themselves get lost. Build bridges of understanding between those who so specialize that they forget the generality and those who think so rarely that they take fright at the unfamiliar, for the sake of him who is not only the Truth but also the Way.

Day Sixteen ◑ *Evening*

Gifts of the Spirit – Wisdom

Wisdom

God save me from cleverness and grant me wisdom.

Wisdom's fruits

O Holy Wisdom, impart to me I pray
    the gift to see the entire picture with myself in it,
    the meaning of the whole and the beauty of the parts,
    the perfection of the end and the values in the process,
    the contribution of the failures to the fullness of the
       success,
    the sharpness of conflict for the enriching of harmony,
    the role of destruction in purifying creation,
    the glory of dying for the finding of life.

Wisdom and folly

God, give me grace to suffer fools gladly, but not folly;
    give a sharp edge to my mind, but not to my
       tongue;
    let me cut quickly through the undergrowth of
       verbiage but hurt no life on the way;
    let me be quick to seize an argument, but slow to
       expose an opponent;
for Christ's sake, who alone is both truth and love.

Anglicanism

The Anglican Communion

Almighty God, by whose providence your Church is moulded in changing patterns from time to time, we thank you for the Anglican Communion as it has emerged from the story of the Anglo-Saxon peoples to become a fellowship of many races and cultures; and we pray that we may accept with joy what you have still in store for us in your creation of a fully catholic Church to be the Body of Christ, for his name's sake.

The Quadrilateral

God of our fathers and our God, we thank you that our gift of heritage is also our calling to fullness in Christ. We thank you for:

scripture as the source of all knowledge necessary for salvation, and we pray for those who continue to expose its inexhaustible treasure;

the faith once delivered to the Saints, and we pray that honest scholarship may deepen our understanding of it;

the sacrament of our birth and nourishment in Christ, and we pray that we may be more and more united by them in holiness;

a three-fold ministry of grace, and pray that it may become the sign of unity instead of the disunity in the Body of Christ.

Day Seventeen ☽ *Evening*

Gifts of the Spirit – Understanding

Understanding

Father, knowledge is fairly accessible; complete it with understanding, for truth's sake.

Both–and/either–or

God, you alone see every side of every question without being paralyzed by doing so. Grant to me the gift of understanding, by which I may see both this side and that, yet still choose, for there are two sides to every question – the right side and the wrong. Only you know for certain which is which, so give me faith, courage and forgiveness, for Christ's sake.

For clarity of feeling

Lord, we are overwhelmed by undisciplined squads of emotion, we are bombarded in print and on TV with random 'feelings'. Grant us the spirit of discipline, so that power and love may prevail over fearfulness, that fearfulness which grips us when we feel lost, for you are the Way, the Truth, the Life.

Day Eighteen ✳ Morning

The Orthodox Tradition

'Sobornost'
(Russian for 'fellowship', or in Greek 'koinonia')

O God, whose nature is universal love, create in us your children, that fellowship in love which shall, at the last, embrace all your creation, in a worship which is our true glory, for Jesus Christ's sake.

Our true glory

God most holy, in worshipping you we discover the glory of humanity, for left to our own devices we become less than human even if we are the most ingenious of beasts. Spare us, Lord, from pride and grant us so to worship you that we may find ourselves, for Christ's sake.

The mystical Body of Christ

Lord Christ, help us to ponder the mystery of the Church as your Body in which:

> one Will moves, though in varied ways in various limbs and organs;
>
> one Mind utters, though in a variety of thoughts and statements;
>
> one Organism is evident for all to see, despite the diverse parts.

Spirit of Christ, lead us into all the truth which we need in order to *be* your Body.

Gifts of the Spirit – Counsel

Counsel

God, let me have the counsel to give, which others would do well to receive.

Shades of grey

O God of pure and uncreated light, in whom is no darkness at all, give me courage never to call black white, and perception to distinguish between shades of grey.

Forgiveness of wrong counsel

Father, forgive me the misdirection I have given to others and enable them to forgive me, by the same grace by which I can forgive those who misled me, namely the Divine Wisdom who corrects us all, sooner or later, even if only in that Last Judgement which is our terror and our hope.

Soul friends

It is not good to be alone. Give to each and all of us, Lord, someone we are glad to trust and the humility to trust them; for you, too, are the friend of sinners.

Day Nineteen ✳ *Morning*

The Catholic Tradition

The Church of Rome

Almighty God, in whose divine providence all sinfulness may be overruled for good, we praise you that, in the division of Christendom, the Catholic Church of the West has borne such fair flowers and fruit, in holiness, zeal and learning. We pray that nothing may be lost and that all may be enriched in the healing of our schisms, according to your holy will, through the Great Shepherd of all your sheep, Jesus Christ our Lord.

Unity not uniformity

Father, we have always recognized that unity is not uniformity, but we are not very good at manifesting true community. Grant to those who love diversity a vision of the common life, and to those who love cohesion a vision of the freedom to differ in our varied settings. For Christ's sake, for he is both our peace and its disturber.

The Holy Father

O God who alone can bear the weight of all your Church, grant to your child, the Pope, such humble dependence on you that, being the servant of the servants of God, he may find the yoke easy and the burden light in the power of Jesus Christ, our common Lord.

Day Nineteen ◐ Evening

Gifts of the Spirit – Spiritual Strength

Spiritual strength

God, grant me faithfulness in small choices, so that I am ready to be faithful in big ones;

> grant me by the daily exercise of moral muscles to be ready, if needed, for heroic action;

> grant that as the body decays, so may the soul be renewed to bear the weight of eternal glory,

through Christ my Saviour.

All the saints and me

It can be done! That is the message of the saints. It can be done:

> the courage that faces martyrdom unflinchingly,
> the patience that endures endless misunderstanding,
> the generosity which throws away all earthly security,
> the love which suffers long and is kind.

Your saints, dear Lord, prove that it can be done. Thanks be to God.

Day Twenty ✳ Morning

The Protestant Tradition

Justification

Help me, O Lord, to give up the futile attempt to justify myself, whether to myself, to others or to you. Let me accept myself as I am because that is the self which you have accepted, and you alone are to be trusted.

'Here I stand'
(Martin Luther)

O God of Truth, grant me grace to know when to stop being tolerant and when to be pig-headed to your glory alone.

A Confessing Church
(The name of the Protestant Christians in Nazi Germany who resisted the state's control of the Church.)

Lord, forgive us that we have other gods than you. We betray, in our acts, that we worship numbers, esteem of self, approval of others, security, relevance and a whole gallery of idols. Make us a Confessing Church, which trusts in Christ and him alone, whatever the cost.

Day Twenty ☽ Evening

Gifts of the Spirit – Knowledge

Knowledge

Lord, let me be a fool for Christ's sake, but not an idiot; simple, but not an ignoramus.

Scholarship

Scholarship is a duty, a trust and a snare: let me labour for knowledge, use it well, and never abuse it.

Prayer in a library

God of all knowledge and truth, I am awed by this reminder of the vast continents of learning, partly explored, mostly unknown. Grant to human minds both a deep humility and an insatiable curiosity, that we may get lost in your infinity only to find that we are at home.

God be in my thinking

Jesus, you are Lord: Lord, you were Jesus. Guide and guard my little mind so that I move between dwelling on what the senses may know and the records of what was seen and heard and handled; and on what eye has not seen nor ear heard of the ineffable mystery of the Eternal Word. Let me behold his glory.

Religious Liberty

Free churches

O God in whom alone we are free, grant to your Church a continuing concern for religious liberty and a passionate rejection of indifference.

Freedom to dissent

O God, where your Spirit is, there is liberty: forgive us when we compel others to go out from our fellowship if they are to be free, and grant to your Church such gifts of the Spirit that there may be freedom to dissent without breaking fellowship or denying truth, through Jesus Christ our Lord, in whom truth and freedom meet.

Quakers

Heavenly Father, author of peace and lover of concord, teach all your people to make for peace and to live in harmony as effectively as does the Society of Friends. Teach us all to be more quiet; give us all to have deeper concerns; and grant to Quakers such insight into the sacramental ways of your working that they may come to love your sacraments, for the sake of Jesus Christ and to the blessing of us all.

Day Twenty-one ☽ Evening

Gifts of the Spirit – Godliness

Godliness

O God, our hearts are restless until they rest in thee,
  our souls are hungry until fed by thee,
  our wills are divided until united with thee.
Give us grace to love what we long to love,
  to do what we long to do,
  to be what we long to be,
  to live in godliness since it is to live in thee,
O God, our Lord and our Redeemer.

The loveliness of God

My God, you are very beautiful; your loveliness surpasses anything I had imagined. And your goodness is breathtakingly lovely. Your saints reflect that beauty; your loveliness in their lives makes this earth a better place. Glory be to our lovely God, for ever.

Day Twenty-two ✳ Morning

Reconciliation within the Church

Church government

Grant to your Church, Almighty God, the wisdom and the humility to adopt those ways of government which let your kingly rule break through our human devices. Guide patriarchs and bishops, assemblies and synods, clergy and laity, that in all exercise of authority in the Church they may serve only the crown rights of our Redeemer, Jesus Christ.

United and reformed

Father of all, we praise you that when we pay the price of union with fellow Christians, you cleanse us in the process. We praise you that when we allow your Spirit to conform us to your will, you truly draw us together. We praise you for those who are living proof that unity reforms and that reformation unites. Forgive us whenever, by not going the whole way in either, we fail in both, for the sake of our Merciful Redeemer.

Day Twenty-two ◑ Evening

Gifts of the Spirit – Godly Fear

Awe and adoration

'His delight shall be in the fear of the Lord' (RSV)
'The fear of Yahweh is his breath.' (JB)
(Isaiah 11:3)

God, who art the mystery, tremendous and fascinating,
keep my soul prostrate in awe until thy gracious word,
and that alone, invites me to lift my face to adore thy
holiness.

'My Lord and my God'
(John 20:28)

Lord, I am always wanting to probe and explore, to
handle the evidence; bring me to my knees with St
Thomas, in holy fear, no longer wanting to touch because
I adore, my Lord and my God.

From fear to trust

Is it fear, Lord, that holds me back from complete abandonment? As those learning to swim fear to trust the
water, as clay may fear the potter's wheel? I can only float
by letting go; I can only be modelled by being passive.
Teach me the necessary trust to allow you to have your
way, which will prove to be my joy.

Christian Unity

'That they may be one'
(John 17:22)

Lord Christ, you are praying for us still:
    that we may be one that the world may believe,
    that we may be sanctified in your word which is truth,
    that we may share your glory which is your cross.
Teach us how to die with you, that with you we may find
new life, in union with your Father and so with each
other.

Christ in Christians

O Christ, very God and very Man, we adore you in one
another; we praise you that in every fellow Christian you
are made manifest, a living sacrament of your Real
Presence.

Inter-communion

Almighty Father, unite us anew to you and to one
another; as we share one bread make us to be one body,
in time as we are in eternity. Grant to us who may not
partake together of the feast at your table to see the day
when the Church on earth shall more fully reflect the
heavenly banquet to which all your children are called by
Jesus Christ, our only Saviour.

Day Twenty-three ☽ *Evening*

The Beatitudes – Blessed are the poor

'For theirs is the kingdom of heaven'
(Matthew 5:3)

Lord, I seem destined to possess things; a large house with much in it, many books and varied clothing, enough money to be delivered from always thinking about it. Grant me, I pray, such detachment from it all that my relationship to my loved ones and to you would be unaffected if all this were to disappear overnight and leave me literally poor and therein blessed, for Christ's sake.

The gifts of time and desire

God, help me to face facts. I am bankrupt. I have nothing with which to face your account when you send it in. But no – you have given me two assets, time and desire. I do not know how much time, except that today seems to be realizable, and there is an unknown number of tomorrows. And desire – I want to fill that time with love for you and for others. Help me to do so better than in the past.

Day Twenty-four * Morning

Evangelism

Evangelization

Father, forgive us that so often those who are zealous to spread the Good News lack sensitivity, and that the sensitive so often lack urgency. Grant to your Church, in all its forms, a gentle persistence which is win-some, for Christ's sake.

Ambassadors for Christ
(2 Corinthians 5:20)

O God, you are in Christ; in Christ you reconcile the world to yourself. You have appointed us to be his ambassadors; you have given to us the ministry of reconciliation. Help me now so to take counsel with my Sovereign that I may share his mind,

so to draw upon his power that I may do his will,
so to love the greatness of his kingdom that I share its vision,
so to be reconciled myself with God that I may be a centre of reconciliation for others.

O Christ my King, with your Father and the Spirit, one God, yours is the kingdom, the power, and the glory for ever.

The Beatitudes – Blessed are they that mourn

'For they shall be comforted'
(Matthew 5:4)

O God of all comfort, grant to those who grieve, whether for sin or for sorrow, that they may so yield to grief that they grow not hard, but, by admitting that they are hurt, may be open to being healed.

Mourning and moping

Teach me, Lord, the difference between moping over what cannot be altered and mourning for what may yet be glorified.

Tears
(Luke 11:35)

Jesus, you wept for Lazarus. Be with those who are in tears; give them some relief as they release their grief. And grant them, through their tears, to see you standing beside them in your risen power.

One God: Three Faiths

One God

Holy God, you are One; the same all through:
    a Father–Creator who is always Christ-like,
    a loving Redeemer who is undefeatable love,
    a mediating Sanctifier who makes us become more like
      Jesus.
One and the same God you always were, are now, and
always will be.

The Jews

Dear Father of all, we give you thanks for the Jews, into
whose race and faith Jesus was born and lived; draw
Christians and Jews closer to each other in this world, as
we will surely be in the world to come.

Muslims

Holy God, for ever One and beyond all reckoning, we
thank you for all who bear you witness. We thank you for
all Muslims; for their disciplined prayer and for their
testimony to your transcendence in purity of life, and in
purity of line in architecture and in calligraphy; for their
austerity of thought and devotion to science. Preserve
them, and us, from all cruel fanaticism and harsh legalism,
and enfold us all in your forgiveness until we see your
face.

The Beatitudes – Blessed are the meek

'For they shall inherit the earth'
(Matthew 5:5)

God give me, when it is needed, the fierce courage of those who have forgotten themselves in devotion to others – that is the meekness which inherits the earth.

'Them that are meek shall he guide ...'
(Psalm 25:8)

O God, by whom the meek are guided in judgement and the gentle are taught thy way, grant to us such self-forgetting trust in thee that we may find thy paths of mercy and truth, for thy name's sake.

Tamed by God
(The Greek for meek means 'a tamed animal'.)

O God whom I serve, let my spirit be strong yet gentle, because I have been tamed by you and by nothing else.

The gift of hospitality

The 'world' reckons that the meek are simply a doormat. But it is always heart-warming to step onto a doormat marked 'welcome'.

Eastern Spirituality

True transcendental meditation

God, you are silence beyond all quietness,
> you are brilliance beyond all light,
> you are tranquility beyond all peace.

Teach me to listen to your silence, let me glimpse your brightness and grant me that tranquility in which the search for you begins.

Yet, none of us could seek if we had not been found
> by the Word who interprets the silence,
> in the Face which reflects your glory,
> through the Passion which is our peace.

Through Jesus Christ, in whom our search begins and in whom it ends, who with you and the Spirit, are the One God in all and through all.

The light of the world

Father of us all, we pray for the millions who seek you by paths other than those we know. Grant to us a charity which accepts them for themselves, and yet never doubts that Jesus loves them enough to want them to meet him.

The Beatitudes – Blessed are the hungry

'For they shall be satisfied'
(Matthew 5:6)

Lord, I have never been really hungry, only just hungry enough to realize how good it can be to taste food.

Let us never forget those whose physical hunger gnaws continually, so that we who have plenty may be instruments of the blessing to them of being satisfied, according to your will.

Daily Bread

'Give us this day our daily bread ...' (Matthew 6:11; Luke 11:3)
'Jesus said, "I am the bread of life".' (John 6:35)
'I am the living bread which has come down from heaven.' (John 6:51)

Lord Christ, you know I have daily needs; I can only live peacefully if I live trustingly, free from fear and the aggression fear brings, from anxiety and the distraction that brings. Lord Christ, you are yourself the deliverer from fear, the answer to anxiety. Please be my daily bread.

Faith World-wide

African Christians

Thank you, Father of all, for the amazing vitality of African Christians;

for their laughter and their joy,

for their dance and exuberance,

for their sense of the Great Spirit underlying and informing all nature and all relationships,

for the swift growth of the Church, especially in its own particular and unique forms.

Through them, Father, enrich us all.

The World Council of Churches

God the Holy Trinity, we worship you in a fellowship from every race and nation, reading the Holy Scriptures in every language, acknowledging one Christ as God and Saviour. Forgive us for letting all this make so little difference to the way we live, and, in your mercy, use this fellowship to manifest your true Church to your glory, Triune and Eternal God.

Other faiths

O God of many names and faces, grant to us who see you in the face of Jesus, to see him in all who long for holiness and eternity.

Day Twenty-seven ☽ *Evening*

The Beatitudes – Blessed are the merciful

'For they shall obtain mercy'
(Matthew 5:7)

Grant me, Lord, to judge others as I would wish to be judged:

> to make excuses for others' failures as I do for my own,
> to believe in others as I need to be believed in,
> to be merciful that I may receive mercy and not what I deserve,

for Christ's sake.

Justice and mercy

God of righteousness, grant us to be just. That in itself would be a great gain, for the world is full of injustice and justice is the social form of love. Yet, alone, it is not enough.

Grant us the generosity which goes further than justice alone requires: in national conflicts, in industrial strife, in class and race struggles. Let new hope be born because people were first just and then generous, for your mercy's sake.

Day Twenty-eight ✳ Morning

Healing

For one who is sick

Lord, [*Name*] whom you love is sick:
Do for [*him/her*] according to [*his/her*] need, dear Lord.

The wounded in psyche

O Christ, thank you for coming among us as the one whole man. Because we have seen you, we do not despair. It is possible to be hurt but not to be destroyed; to feel abandoned but not to be lost for ever. We pray you to reach through to those who are so deeply hurt in mind that they are desperate; so long defeated that they have lost hope. Let them see and feel that they are accepted by the Rejected One – and so find peace and be surprised by joy.

Preach the Gospel, heal the sick
(*Luke 9:1–6*)

Lord, we falter before your commands. We do not truly believe that you make whole, that your kingdom comes when brokenness is healed. Give to your Church, in all its parts and in all its ministries, a renewed faith in your healing power, that broken bones may rejoice!

The Beatitudes – Blessed are the pure in heart

'For they shall see God'
(Matthew 5:8)

O God, who art of purer eyes than to behold iniquity, make my heart one upon which thou mayest look, that I may become one who may look upon thee, for Christ's sake.

Pure in heart

O God, I would see you; grant me then that purity of heart which is the only ground of such a blessing.

The primal vision

Father, there is a way of seeing which is given to children and other blessed ones; it notices much but is never confused by details; it picks out essentials amidst the flourishes. Give me fresh eyes, so that I may see what I now miss.

Contemplative prayer

I AM who made you, calls you and awaits you; still your restless spirit by gentle dwelling upon himself alone, until his breath is yours.

Peace

Peace negotiators

God, strengthen those who work at the details of coexistence in a torn world, who have sat for years round the same conference tables and seen few results; let them share in your endless patience, and in your inflexible will, for Christ's sake.

A prayer for disarmament

Lord, here is your cross: you must bear it alone.
It is too hard for us; we need other defences.
It is too simple; we must have our own strategists.
We know all the arguments; we never hear yours.
Lord argue with us; show us new ways.
Get us out of this situation which we have landed
    ourselves in,
For your world's sake.

Peace in industry

Lord, we confess that social justice is sometimes rough justice; conflicting interests battle for power. Grant to those who are tempted to ever-increasing intransigence the grace to glimpse the wisdom of compromise in struggles where no one can 'win', for your pity's sake.

Day Twenty-nine ● Evening

The Beatitudes – Blessed are the peacemakers

'For they shall be called children of God'
(Matthew 5:9)

Prince of Peace, help us to see that peace is not easily come by; it has to be made, and often at great cost. Send us into the world ready to pay the price of making peace, so that we may be called the children of God, in union with you who paid so high a price for the peace of the world.

Personal peacemakers

God, we thank you for the healing work of counsellors, bringing self-knowledge; for the insights of psychiatrists, restoring mental peace; for the guidance of confessors, assuring the peace of sins forgiven; and for all those whom you use to plant your peace in the lives of your people, for Christ's sake.

War and conflict

One and only God of all humanity, by whatever name we call you, have mercy on us all. We call to you in anguish for the sins we have all committed, and still commit against each other. Bring to nothing the power of those who hate, and bring to fruit the desire of the peace-makers, the true children of God.

Justice

The law

O God, grant us such laws that
   the innocent may be protected,
   the tempted may be deterred, and
   the guilty may be redeemed;
for Christ's sake.

The police

Protect those who protect us;
   protect them from the malice of others,
   protect them from the anger inside themselves,
   protect them from deserving abuse,
and give them grace to bear what they do not deserve, as
Jesus did.

JPs and judges

God, in Christ you have forbidden us to judge, lest we be
judged; yet you have also committed to some the
mediated reflection of your own eternal righteousness.
Guard those who carry that aweful burden, that, knowing
themselves to be sinners, they may seek mercy whilst they
mete justice, and seek forgiveness whilst they deal punish-
ment, for Christ's sake.

The Beatitudes – Blessed are the persecuted

'For theirs is the kingdom of heaven'
(Matthew 5:10)

Father, we pray with admiration in our hearts for those who suffer persecution for Christ's sake. We pray for those who are imprisoned, that, in the loss of one freedom, they may find another. We pray for those in exile, that, in losing their homeland they may discover the citizenship which you alone confer. We pray for those whose persecution is through a host of irksome slights and mean deprivations, that they may be strengthened in humour and toughened by grace. Grant that we, seeing that the kingdom of heaven is theirs, may be glad for them and prepare ourselves to be thus blessed.

When words hurt

Lord, we do not believe it. When people 'speak all manner of evil against' us, we are resentful or hurt or indignant, and we say that it is because 'the Church is misrepresented'. Let us rather search our hearts to see whether it is because we are truly in the tradition of the prophets who were persecuted before us. If so, may we rejoice; if not, help us to keep quiet.

Discipleship

Religious communities

O God, you ask of us all that we have, that we may be united with you; pour your blessings especially upon those who have responded to your calling with a more thorough abandonment than most and, in their close commitment to each other, reward them with closeness to you.

The three vows made my own
(Poverty, chastity and obedience)

O God, give me complete freedom from dependence
 upon the things of which I am a steward, so
 that if they went it would make no real
 difference.

Give to all my relationships that appropriateness
 to the persons concerned, so that none of
 them may do other than draw me nearer to
 you.

Give me such abandonment to your will that I
 may be obedient to your authority, whoever
 may be used to convey it.

For Christ's sake.

Christian Perfection

Christian perfection

(Revelation 14:1, 22:4)

Holy Father, let me share your holiness. Yet that will come not by seeking it but only by seeking you.
Burn out of me by *your* holiness all that would make *my* holiness into a possession of mine.
Write my new name on my forehead where only others can see it.

Grace and truth

Jesus, Lord of all grace and truth,
grant that grace may bring us to you,
and that truth may keep us there,
for ever and ever, for your Name's sake.

'Be ye therefore perfect'

(Matthew 5:48)

Heavenly Father, as I contemplate the loveliness of creation I glimpse how lovely must be the Creator; take me now, a part of your creation, and mould me nearer to that perfection for which you made me. Let my whole being praise you, as birds and flowers do in their way, ever more fully here and completely hereafter, for Christ's sake.

Occasional Prayers

Suffering

Patience in sickness

O God of infinite patience, give your patience to us when we grow weary of uncertain health; help us to know both the humility which accepts limitations and the confidence which never despairs, for the sake of him who endured the cross.

Pain

Almighty God, Creator and Saviour, I thank you for pain as a warning that something is wrong and may perhaps be cured. I do not ask to be spared pain, but I do ask for the courage to bear it. I thank you for the applied knowledge which can alleviate it, and I pray that I may never forget that it was in pain that our redemption was won, on the cross of our Lord Jesus.

Acceptance of Diminishment

Lord, there comes a point when all powers diminish: I am growing slower, stupider, weaker, less alive. Grant me to accept this with fortitude – but with more than fortitude. It is good to be brave but it is better to be joyful. All this experience of diminishment can also be a joyful discovery that your strength is made perfect in weakness.

Sharing the darkness

Dear Lord, you are specially close to us when we are dying, perhaps more so when we cannot feel you near.

You are specially close to those who care continually for the dying, perhaps more so when they are tired out.

Grant to both the cared-for and the carers an awareness of your closeness that will lighten the darkness enough to make all the difference, just when they need it most, for Jesus' sake.

Through tears

Teach us all that there are times when we can *only* see you through our tears.

Joy cometh in the morning
(Psalm 30:5)

Dear Father, some nights can be very dark. Night-time can last a long while, but 'joy cometh in the morning'. Help me to believe that, even during the longest nights, for you are the day-spring, my joy.

Work

Being busy

'To be busy is to be engaged in an occupation which makes it inconvenient to be disturbed.' (Mother Janet Stuart)

Father, forgive the many times when I have resented being disturbed; grant me, next time, an instant assessment to weigh what I am doing against what I am asked to do.

Feeling indispensable

'Keep your servant also from presumptuous sins, lest they get dominion over me.' (Psalm 19:13)

Lord, I am tempted to think myself indispensable; I work too hard because I do not really trust you or anyone else. Keep your servant from these presumptuous sins lest they get dominion over me, and I discover, too late, that I have lost humility. For the sake of him who blessed the meek, Jesus, my only Saviour.

In your service

O Lord, forgive me for the pride which leads to excess of zeal, and the sloth into which I react after it. Grant me the temperance which is content to be worn out in your service, but slowly and wisely, for the sake of him who set his face steadfastly to go up to Jerusalem, Jesus, our Lord.

The Caring Professions

Pastoral care

God, you have much to concern you: all creation through all time, and more that we cannot picture.

Yet when I become aware of you, it is as though I alone mattered to you.

Help us, who are concerned with others, to care for them one by one, as though each were the only one, as indeed each is, unique to you, to themselves and to me.

Let me love each as such – and attend accordingly, for Christ's sake.

Social welfare

O God, who shows us love and justice in total harmony, we praise you for all advances in social justice through the welfare state, and we beg you always to send us those who reveal new needs to challenge us, and who find the people who have been forgotten, in the spirit of Jesus, the ceaselessly seeking Shepherd.

The Environment

The garden and the city

God, you began our human life in a garden and will consummate it in a city. Grant that meanwhile we may design the places of our habitation with the humility of gardeners and with the daring of architects, so that we may be fully human.

Farmers

God, we thank you for those whose industry on the land enables us all to be fed. Keep them close to the mystery of creation, so that they may not abuse their power for easy profits. Give to the rest of us such respect for true husbandry that we do not put them under pressure to sin against their Creator and ours.

Working with God

O God, whose creation shows such patient skill in bringing your work to perfection in the phenomenon of man, teach us to be fellow-workers with you, by showing the co-operation which is our highest dignity.

Worship

Music in worship

God of all beauty and joy,
we praise you for the heritage of holy song,
we praise you for soaring voices and heavenly harmony,
we thank you for all hymn-writers and composers who
have enriched our common worship. Alleluia.

A unique offering

Lord, help each of us to discover the unique creative gift
that is ours, so that we may know that each praises you as
no one else can do.

The local church

God, we need our local loyalties. County and country
guard us against being lost in anonymity. Show us how
our worship may have a local accent without becoming
to others a foreign tongue, for the sake of Jesus of
Nazareth.

Justice

Compassion first

Merciful God, give me to feel compassion first of all, in every conceivable setting: to feel the pain of the universe
   in every swatted fly or a cat toying with a mouse;
   in the aggression of the insecure and the stammer of the shy;
   in the hurt of the betrayed and the ignored.
It must not stop there, but whatever ought to be done next is more likely to be right if compassion came first.

Judgement and mercy

Lord God of Israel, you are no compromiser; your demands are unconditional and your standards are absolute.

Lord God of Israel, you are also full of compassion and of great mercy; you know how easily we confuse our wilfulness with your holy will.

Grant to all those who wield power so to attend to your judgement that they discern righteousness, and to your mercy that they discern when others are right. For the sake of him who loves sinners as much as he condemns sin, Jesus Christ, our just and merciful Saviour.

Politics

Tyrants

O God, we pray for those who have seized power by force and who sustain it by fear. Deliver them from their loneliness, so that they may meet their fellow humans and listen to them. Deliver them from fear, that they may learn to share power; and if they are overthrown, deliver them from the hell they carry within themselves, for the sake of him whom Herod sought to kill, our merciful Lord and Christ.

Widen our hearts

'You are restricted in your own affections ... widen your hearts also.' (2 Corinthians 6:12–13)

Loving Father, we praise you for a thawing of your frozen people, a widening of narrow loves and a meekness which does not feel threatened by the strange. Deepen these graces in us all, for the sake of your generous Son, Jesus our Lord.

World Peace

O God, we need peace; how greatly we need it:
   peace in Africa – dear God grant it,
   peace in the Middle East – dear God grant it,
   peace in Northern Ireland – dear God grant it,

peace between the great powers – dear God grant it,
peace between the races – dear God grant it,
peace within human hearts everywhere
and, in each case, only one way to reach it – 'in his will is
our peace'.

Paternoster Pondered

Some extracts on prayer and how to pray, from an unfinished meditation on the Lord's Prayer.

'Lord, teach us to pray ...' (Luke 11:1)

Our Father

The very first word of the Lord's Prayer reminds me that there is never merely 'private prayer'. All prayer is in community, in fellowship: a central Christian experience, what the Greek calls *koinonia*, the Russian *sobornost*.

So, Father, since I often need to pray alone, I find it helpful to begin by naming those for whom I later intercede, to picture them beside me as I say '*Our* Father'.

Then, too, I can base a whole philosophy, a whole world view, on that first word.

You are the Father of all – without distinction of religion, race or colour, of class or status – we are all your children, Father, whether we know it or not. Oh, I know that there is a sense in which Jesus is your only Son by right – but you have adopted us all in him as your children. He, the eternal and only-begotten Son of God, becomes one of us, takes each of us by the hand to lead us to you, Our Father.

Jesus *knew* you as Father; we have to learn it. The Gospel is the news that this is the truth about ourselves.

So this becomes the truly ecumenical prayer, the universal prayer. Often in meetings where many races and nations were represented, I have heard the Lord's Prayer said 'each in his own tongue'. We knew that we were saying something very important, about God and about ourselves, as we said '*Our* Father ...'.

Our *Father*

What word did you use when you gave us the 'Our Father'? Was it the same as you used in that terrible moment in Gethsemane? Struggling with the fate you saw approaching, you prayed 'Abba, Father, all things are possible to thee; remove this cup from me; yet not what I will but what thou wilt' (Mark 14:36).

Many scholars believe that Jesus here took the normal, affectionate, family word of a child and applied it daringly to God. The only adequate translation of abba would be daddy. Dare we say 'dearest dad – in heaven'? Certainly the Church's liturgical tradition has not dared to say it.

I remember, as a very small boy in the First World War, being terrified as I lay in bed in the nearly dark bedroom, that 'a German' was threatening me at the nursery door. My father (home on leave from France) heard my screams. He came upstairs, picked me up in his arms and carried me to the door so that I could feel that the dreaded figure was only my dressing-gown hanging up there!

Daddy in heaven, I find that you still quiet my fears by showing me the truth.

'When we say "Abba, Father" it is the Spirit himself bearing witness with our spirit that we are children of God' (Romans 8:16). So, all at once I find that I am praying in the Blessed and Holy Trinity! This is not some abstract and abstruse doctrine, but simply a vivid and obvious experience. I couldn't get there on my own. The go-between God, the Holy Spirit, has picked me up and I find myself in the strong arms of the Father, and I look into his face, and see the face of Jesus, the human face of God.

Our Father, who art in heaven

There, Lord, is the whole mystery of prayer – the union of
   the near and the far,
   the intimate and the ultimate,
   the familiar and the unknown,
   the most natural and the most strange,
– the traffic between earth and heaven.

That is why prayer is both easy and hard, both a spontaneous response of every human soul and a life-long discipline.

Heaven is home because that is where you, my Father, live. Can I need any further assurance of its loveliness and its reality? As I grow in intimacy with you, as I warm to your presence, so I only long to be where you are always and completely 'at home'.

All created beauty which I have learned here to love – sunshine and moonlight, trees and flowers, the whole rich panorama of nature – all are but foretastes, hints, promises of the beauty of the Creator in his own dwelling-place. It is the logic of love that creation cannot be less lovely than the Creator, the gift less desirable than the Giver.

Lord, open my eyes to the vision of heaven; grant to me to glimpse by faith something more lovely than this world, because it is the home of the author of all loveliness. 'Eye hath not seen, nor ear heard, neither have entered into the heart of man, the things which God hath prepared for them that love him' (1 Corinthians 2:9).

Let me be silent in the face of the immensity of the distance, of this difference, between where I am and where you are. And yet it is your *nearness* which is so mysterious ... 'nearer than breathing' ...

Open my heart to a worship which holds together the ultimate and the intimate.

Hallowed be thy Name

'Holy' is at once the hardest religious word to understand and the most necessary: hard because the holy is the wholly other – that which I am not by nature, that which I cannot control or comprehend, that before which I can worship and adore. It is necessary because without it there is no true religion, only ethics or formal cult. So to say 'Hallowed be thy Name' is first to say 'Let God be God'.

Father, you are holiness or you are nothing.

Father, let my every thought be worthy of you. No, my little mind cannot even conceive a thought that would be worthy of your love, your beauty, your holiness. But at least let me not desecrate your name by thoughts which contradict your Holy Name.

O God, we desecrate your name whenever we think and act as if you were cruel and callous, petty or spiteful. We desecrate your name, Holy Father, whenever we project our own prejudices into the heavens and suppose that the way things are, the pattern of reality itself, is other than the self-sacrificing love you show in Jesus.

Piling up armaments of indiscriminate destruction, squandering food while others starve, exploiting your lovely planet for immediate gain – in all these and a thousand other ways, we desecrate instead of hallowing your name.

Thy kingdom come

You were not crucified, Lord Jesus, for your private religious beliefs but because you threatened the whole public order of things. You did not only offer a new personal relationship with God but you demanded submission to God's rule over every facet of society. God's 'kingdom' is the sphere of his rule.

In you, Lord Christ, and in you alone, two strains in Scripture are reconciled: the present reality – expressed in Jesus the Messiah, the obedient Son who calls his disciples to obedience, and so to share with him in pointing to 'the signs' of the kingdom's presence; and the future vindication of God as king of all – life only makes sense if, some day, all creation demonstrates your rule for all to see. So the kingdom is both now and yet to come …

The Old and New Testaments show us your truth from many different angles. To us many truths may appear incompatible; but in you, Lord Jesus, *all* truth is revealed. In this, surely, lies the true basis of Christian toleration, that 'catholicity' which derives from acknowledging that your truth always exceeds any one formulation of it. Therefore, if we are to be your disciples, we cannot acquiesce in any sectarianism or fanaticism. Help us so to pray that we may see the *end*, and work back from there to here.

O Risen Lord, I bask in the warm knowledge that you reign, that your kingdom is the ultimate assurance that all is well. May I let my own little life find its significance in that grand design. May your kingdom come ...

Thy will be done

Dear Lord, your life on earth was wrapped in obedience. 'Not my will but thine be done' you prayed in Gethsemane – and so you went to your death (Luke 22:42).

As our eternal High Priest, still you say 'Lo, I have come to do thy will, O God' (Hebrews 10:7).

And so, Father, there may be no escape from obedience to your will if I want to walk with Jesus, if I want also to be one of the disciples who watch his long agony in Gethsemane. In the end, is there any other prayer than this – 'Not my will but thine be done'?

Do with me what you will.

Whatever you do, I thank you:

I am ready for all, I accept all.

Let only your will be done in me, and all your creatures.

I wish no more than this, Heavenly Father.

Into your hands I commend my soul. I offer it to you
with all the love I can.

For I *do* love you, in spite of all the failures. I do love you,
and need to give myself to you; to surrender myself
without reserve into your hands, in complete trust, for
you are my Father.